Essential Jobs

We Need Education Workers

by Brienna Rossiter

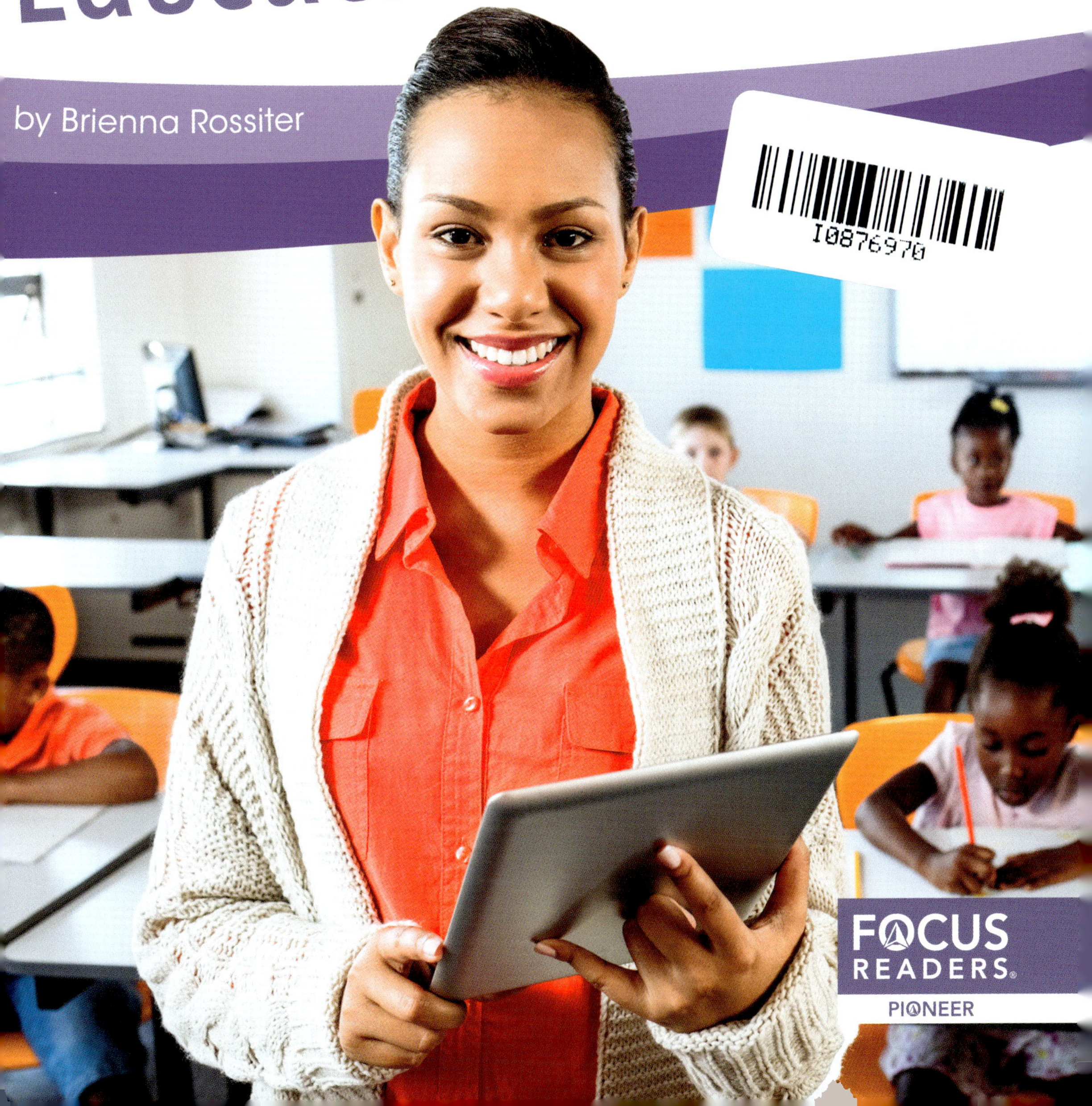

FOCUS READERS

PIONEER

www.focusreaders.com

Focus Readers is distributed by North Star Editions:
sales@northstareditions.com | 888-417-0195

Produced for Focus Readers by Red Line Editorial.

Photographs ©: Shutterstock Images, cover, 1, 4, 7, 8, 11, 12, 15, 17, 18, 21 (top), 21 (bottom)

Library of Congress Cataloging-in-Publication Data
Library of Congress Cataloging-in-Publication Data is available on the Library of Congress website.

ISBN
978-1-63739-029-0 (hardcover)
978-1-63739-083-2 (paperback)
978-1-63739-190-7 (ebook pdf)
978-1-63739-137-2 (hosted ebook)

Printed in the United States of America
Mankato, MN
012022

About the Author

Brienna Rossiter is a writer and editor who lives in Minnesota.

Table of Contents

Chapter 1

Education

People learn in many ways. They can take classes at schools or libraries. They can also work with **tutors** or coaches.

Education workers help make all these things possible. Some education workers teach children. Others work with adults. But they all help people learn and grow.

Fun Fact

Some people plan **field trips**. They help students learn and have fun.

Chapter 2

Caring for Children

Some education workers have jobs at day cares. They teach and care for babies and young children. That way, the parents can go to work.

Other workers teach at preschools. They help kids get ready for school. Kids learn to share and work together.

Kids also learn about letters. This helps them **prepare** to read. Kids learn numbers, too. This helps them learn math.

Chapter 3

Working at Schools

Many people teach and work in schools. Some teachers focus on just one **subject**. For example, they may teach art or science. Others teach the same group of students all day.

Other workers help the school run. These workers help plan school events. They choose how the school will spend money. They also help with **discipline**.

Fun Fact

A principal is in charge of all the students and teachers at a school.

Special Ed

Special ed teachers help schools meet the needs of all students. First, they learn each student's needs. Then, they plan how to help. Some students may need extra time to take tests. Others may need help with reading. Some special ed teachers have their own classrooms. Some work with small groups.

Chapter 4

In the Community

People can learn in many places outside schools. They can visit museums. They can go to zoos. Workers there make **displays**. They also plan activities.

Other people work at libraries. Librarians help visitors find books. They help visitors do **research**. They also plan the library's events. Many libraries have clubs or classes for people.

Fun Fact

Some libraries have **makerspaces**. In these areas, people can build things.

FOCUS ON

Education Workers

Write your answers on a separate piece of paper.

1. Write a sentence describing one job that education workers do.
2. If you were a teacher, what subject would you teach? Why?
3. Which type of workers help people find books or do research?
   - A. principals
   - B. librarians
   - C. field trips
4. Why would learning about letters help prepare kids to learn how to read?
   - A. Reading is about words, which are made of letters.
   - B. Reading is about math, which uses letters.
   - C. Reading is not taught in most schools.

Answer key on page 24.

Glossary

discipline
Training people to follow rules and correcting people who break those rules.

displays
Groups of signs and objects that people can look at and learn from.

field trips
Times when groups of students travel to a place, such as a zoo, to learn about it.

makerspaces
Places with tools and supplies that people can use to create or invent things.

prepare
To get ready.

research
Learning more about something.

subject
A type of class in school. Reading, science, and math are common subjects.

tutors
People who help small groups of students work on a specific skill, such as reading.

To Learn More

BOOKS

Gaertner, Meg. *Librarians*. Minneapolis: Abdo Publishing, 2019.

Meinking, Mary. *Teachers*. North Mankato, MN: Capstone Publishing, 2020.

NOTE TO EDUCATORS

Visit **www.focusreaders.com** to find lesson plans, activities, links, and other resources related to this title.

Index

Answer Key: 1. Answers will vary; **2.** Answers will vary; **3.** B; **4.** A